AF323337

MEMORIES THAT BURN AND BLESS

Other books by this Author:
The Searching Season
Fling Jeweled Pebbles
Selections from the Searching Season
The Wood Burns Red
Cry Before Dawn

Also, a long-playing album *The Wood Burns Red and Other Poems* by Roberta Goldstein

MEMORIES THAT BURN AND BLESS

By

Roberta Butterfield Goldstein

THE GOLDEN QUILL PRESS
Publishers
Francestown   New Hampshire

Library of Congress Catalog Card Number 84-90360

ISBN 0-8233-0385-3

Printed in the United States of America

DEDICATED

to the memory
of Harold M. Levin   d. 1947
and Frank Goldstein   d. 1982
and to their living legacy
Harold Michael Levin Goldstein
Mark Kingston Levin Goldstein
Jan Mordecai Goldstein
Ethel Faith Goldstein Wright

ACKNOWLEDGEMENTS

Grateful acknowledgement and thanks are made to the editors of the following magazines in which some of these poems first appeared: *The Mountain Troubadour, Second Harvest Anthology of the Poetry Society of Vermont, Cyclo-Flame, Avalon Dispatch, Poet, Ocarina, Encore, Driftwood East, Sandcutters* and *The Jewish Spectator.*

''The Gift'' was reprinted in *The Pen Woman,* ''Shattered Sabbath'' was reprinted in the *Anthology of Magazine Verse & Yearbook of American Poetry* (1981), and ''Lines to Bat Sheva'' will be reprinted in the 1984 edition of this Anthology.

A million thanks to my daughter-in-law Cheryl Allard Goldstein whose professional expertise in the preparation of my manuscript for presentation to the publisher is deeply appreciated.

CONTENTS

MEMORIES THAT BURN AND BLESS

BURN AND BLESS

The earth turns
unfeelingly upon its axis
as predictable
as sun and moonrise.

The fire burns
in every sumac and maple
at this torched turning
of the harvest season.

The blood churns
when wild geese pause in flight
and dare to seek haven
upon a mirror-pond.

A woman learns
that loneliness exacts a price
in memories that burn
and bless, bless and burn.

The heart still yearns
the earth turns
while memories like leaves
blaze brightly
yet they are *not* consumed.

OF ALL THE MONTHS

We were always closest in September
when the smells of ripening fruit
perfume the air,
and a curious blend
of late summer heat
tinged with the crisp coolness of fall
tangs nose and heart
with pungent poignancy.
We stole time for long walks
in the fields and late picnics
under burning maple and burnished oak.
I remember how fast we would run
to the top of the highest hill,
and watch the unscrolling of an autumn
sunset more colorful
than all the pageantry
of coronations!

September was the month wherein
we always lived and loved the best.
How strange it turned
into a month of mourning
that September
you were laid to rest.

BROTHER-FATHER-HERO

My brother and I, born a decade apart,
often seemed to enact
our separate fairy tale.
I played the ''Princess of Make-Believe.''
and he, the ''Red-headed Elf of Devious Deeds.''
He eavesdropped on my most secret
conversations, stole my diary,
emptied pocketbook and piggy bank,
and harassed my every friend.
Once, as a Princess Incognito,
I was carrying two glass bottles of milk,
he jumped out at me from the darkness!
The bottles clanged and shattered—
my crown fell into a flood of milk and glass.

When my anger dissolved,
I looked at my brother—
my heart aching for him.
Sadly, I knew that he could never
remember father the way I did.
I had hoarded every fresh minted moment.
My brother could remember only a man,
shrunken by illness—
waxen in death. A passing shadow.
FOREVER, I hugged close to me
the memory of a tall hero,
who had always slain
the dreadful dragons
breathing fire

SWEET SEPTEMBER

The bronze and orange marigolds nestle
like colored eggs in the blue rice bowl,
gracing the polished table.
I set a place for one.

My hands feel strange not to set
your placemat across from me.
The tea kettle whistles merrily—
steamy notes of cheer.
One steak broils,
I cut salad greens.
My eyes mist and I can feel
your breath as you kiss my cheek.
Instinctively, I reach out
to touch your face—
my fingers caress
empty air.
The china clock ticks the minutes
of sweet September,
our month for rejoicing.
Everywhere I move,
I smell the spice of marigolds,
and always hear the echo
of your resonant,
familiar voice.

GROWING UP

Once when I was a child too small to touch
the tall golden walls of the morning,
Daddy built a house for Mother and me,
a large white house full of sun,
and a big play yard that smelled
of peonies or roses all summer long.
For our lively horses, he built shining stables.
I called my own white stallion, ''Prince'';
he bucked the hired man, but always nuzzled me.
One flowering day, Daddy surprised me with a pair
of rabbits, one all black and his mate white,
they were velvet soft and cuddly with wiggly ears.

In late summer when we visited my grandparents,
the telephone rang and rang! Mother bundled me up
and hustled me out to our Model T. I fell asleep.
The sun glared red and hot, I awoke and knew
we were home. We climbed out of the car—
I looked and looked—gone were our house and
    stables—
they were not anywhere—burned to the ground.
Nothing left—only the chimney leaning
amid thin trails of choking smoke,
and black cinders flying everywhere.

Our neighbors had saved the horses,
but forgot my rabbits.
Waves of nausea flooded me—
''throwing up'' could not ease the emptiness.

From that moment
I felt that anything
could never be min
no matter how beau
or dearly beloved.

HER PROTE

She strode ahead pu
for several minutes,
then she stopped abr
as if by a stop watch.
Hesitantly, she stoope
to pick a deep blue ge
and then she heard the
singing hymns of prais
to their Invisible Make
The loneliness in her th
burned like hot dry dust
She had no desire
to laud the One
who had bereft her twice
of a beloved mate.
Let the sparrows
searching for crumbs
and anticipating rain rejoic
She would utter no blasphe
her only protest would be
one silent voice.

in the enchanted woods
of my childhood.

PAPER ROSES

Mother loved the crimson roses blooming
with green leaves on her bedroom wall.
In summer, they brought the garden in,
and when the snow came, they kept the winter
out. I can still see her in these cold days
at sunset, as she ran from room to room,
gleaning from each window
the last gold glint of sun.
Those sunsets when she gathered gold
and the red, red roses growing
upon her chamber wall,
helped Mother to keep sane
in the seasons of her loneliness.
Night after night, we heard her
crying softly, as her empty arms
hugged the feather pillow
where Daddy's head had always lain,
when life held much more
than paper roses blooming
in a garden on the wall.

VANISHED

Today I turned around
and our summer was gone.
Oh, to be sure,
children still wiggled their toes
in the late warm sand
and roses still bloomed
in mother's garden,
but now and then
when the wind blew cold
they shivered
both roses and children.
I longed to race with you
up the east hill
to the grove of pines,
but the sun didn't shine
and you were nowhere
we'd ever been.
I asked all over the neighborhood,
nobody had seen you.
I thought you might have hidden
in our secret wood
where grown-ups were forbidden.
I was looking and looking
(until my knees were sore)
for a lucky four-leaf-clover
when I heard it!
The piercing whistle
of the vanished train
and knew you had fled

like summer
unconquered
and unconcerned
that all my fingers bled.

DOUBLE CINQUAIN

Fall rain
touches my face
suddenly you appear
tears and rain mingle with kisses
love drenched.

Sunset
burnt orange sky
multi-colored carpet
on whirling earth we two touch sky
sprout wings.

THE FINE LINE

Mother didn't tell me
that life isn't truly
just like a fairy tale,
that frogs always fail
to turn into princes,
and bright red apples
often taste like quinces.

Never did she hint
that living
"Happily ever after"
has the somber tint
of hidden grief
whose hollow laughter
lies like a thief.

Mother didn't tell me
how I should learn
to distinguish between
the "real" and fantasy.
Now, blindfolded, I turn
and painfully feel
my uncertain course
across the fine line
of "once upon a time."

THE GIFT

Grandmother told me never to give
my heart to a man
who whipped his horse
or cursed his dog, or
who gave only dry kisses,
or carried an umbrella
for a stroll in summer rain.

Grandmother told me to give
my heart when I found a love
as warm as hot flat irons
wrapped in flannel
on a cold winter night,
and as faithful as the flame
of a freshly trimmed kerosene lamp,
and gentle as the sleep
of two who lie in the center
of a voluminous feather bed.

Ten years have passed since
Grandmother said her last good-bye.
Today I took the deep purple lilacs
my husband gave me for our anniversary
along with coffee kisses,
and placed them on grandmother's grave.
I knelt to thank her for advice well taken,
and richly spent.

MY MORTAL ENEMY

All my clocks are running down,
I shall refuse to wind them.
Let me celebrate this day,
unblemished, unchimed, yet urgent!
I long to caress
the damask texture
of this gentle moment,
and savor its mellow wine,
while I bask in the hush
of an untimed hour.
In the velvet evening,
I will walk upside down,
and inhale the fragrance
of moonlit orchards,
bountiful with blossoms
of apple, pear and plum.

When I return at midnight
to wind my clocks again,
I shall pretend *not* to mind,
that time, my mortal enemy,
grows more and more unkind.

NO LONGER MOLASSES BOUND

The years fall like a house of cards,
today becomes tomorrow
before I've even savored the now.
Yesterday was a carousel,
and I climbed off my horse
before the music stopped,
but you stayed on,
and went around and around,
all of your rides were for free.
I wanted to climb back on,
and feel the pony go up and down,
but my feet seemed stuck in the ground,
as if I stood in taffy molasses.
Somewhere vesper bells were ringing,
yet the only sound I wanted to hear
was the tinkling upside-down tune,
as the carousel spun around and around.
You shouted at the top of your voice:
''See me standing in the saddle!''
As usual you were a flamboyant show-off
and I, your captive audience,
clapped hands like a mechanical doll.

I've moved in my own direction
no longer molasses bound,
you still linger, my friend,
on the tinkling merry-go-round.

SEPTEMBER SOUNDS

A mother's memory awakens
at the ringing of the school bells—
again she sees her small son
scuffing his new shoes
against the curbstone.
Not knowing what school
might be about,
he squeezes her hand
reluctant to let go.
Heart aching beyond reason,
she firmly unclasped
his sticky fingers,
and shoved him through the door
into his sowing season.

Now the small son is a man grown,
a husband and a father
eagerly beginning a new life
in a far off country
with his daughters and wife.
What could a mother do?

Only endure the exquisite pain
of finally letting go.

THE HEALING

A little boy once told my grieving friend,
"See how the flower grows upon the hill."
She looked, and found that death is not the end.
Although the voice of her beloved is still—
In the gentle tapping of falling rain,
In the touch of rough or soft, silken wind,
She can feel him near, and know the raw pain
He bore has fled. Even grief will be thinned
When flowers, hidden beneath the melting snow,
Will rise and bloom as spring awakes from sleep.
Plump robins will replace the raucous crow,
And she who grieves for him will cease to weep.

More powerful than any engine's thrust,
Is man's soul that soars above the body's dust!

VERMONT LEGACY
(In Memory of Alfred H. Butterfield)

I will remember always, Grandfather,
how you held your head high,
even when you were eighty-one,
even when you buried your eldest son,
and your youngest took his life
on your seventieth birthday.
You wore the stripes of sorrow
proudly as Joseph wore his coat
of multi-colors.
An agnostic by choice,
you were no stranger to the
house of God, although
you never tasted the grape
or unleavened bread.
A preacher ranting of hellfire
and damnation, you quickly
tuned out. Yet, one who spoke of the need
for action for social justice,
deeply stirred your soul.

Forever, Grandfather, I will remember
your soft mustachioed kisses,
the gentle warmth of your voice.

I see you now in your printer's cap,
as you sat in the maroon plush rocking-chair,
where you studied with the zeal
of a classical scholar.

The knowledge you culled
from your self-taught studies
could make a University graduate
quite envious.

With the disciplined precision
gained in your youthful days
as craftsman and carpenter,
your hands still moved
with agility as you typed

The news at eighty for the paper
you purchased at the turn
of the century, and named
Palladium and News in honor
of the new town of Troy.

After we buried my father,
beloved physician, cut down
in early autumnal glory
like a scarlet maple
felled by a careless axe,
it was your voice and your arms
that comforted me.
"Cry as much as you like,"
you told me, "you'll learn
that tragedy also brings
a lesson in healing."

The years have fallen like the apples
we once shook from the crab apple

in your dooryard, yet memories endure.
On your golden wedding day, you gave
Grandmother wild roses and honeysuckle,
then with a courtly bow, you kissed her
with the ardor of a newly-wed.

Now you both lie side by side, and above
you as you wished is the granite step
that bore the footprints of all
who entered your cherished home.

Oh, Grandfather, I treasure
your incorruptible spirit,
the lingering gentleness
of your strong arms,
and your soft mustachioed kisses.

NO FRAME COULD HOLD

I thought that love could be kept in a frame
Like the luminous girl with heart-shaped face,
And the tall, lean man who gave her his name—
Mother and Father whose eyes and embrace
Hint of dreams and hopes that never came right.
I gaze at their photo and painfully feel
Their dream world and mine have vanished from
   sight.
Daylight has stripped make-believe from the real.

In sorrow, I've learned love can never be bound,
For a lover resents both fetters and fence;
Love's riches can not be weighed by the pound,
Why did you weigh me in dollars and cents?
No frame could hold all the love I offered you,
Why did you give me only rosemary and rue?

TO THE IMAGE IN THE LOOKING GLASS

You and I have had our ups and tumble-downs.
The carousel has sometimes turned too fast,
We've had our share of smiles and hurtful frowns,
We could not make the candied apples last.
Although the brass ring whirls beyond our reach,
We still have hope when sunshine disappears.
We find the Dream defies the glibbest speech
When stars return to lighten painful fears.
Those awesome goblins fade to fleeing ghosts,
As distant chimes foretell a fresh new start.
Strange shadows cast are nothing more than posts.
Long night has lost its frightened, lonely heart!

The stormy winds have now begun to shift,
Beginnings bring the most unusual gift.

VERMONTER, NINETY YEARS YOUNG
(for Anne H. Butterfield)

My Mother sifts the days, weeks, months and
  years
as vigorously as she has always sifted
the flour for her fresh green-apple pies.
Mother spends no time wasting fruitless tears
for her brave ones who have slowly drifted
past the last port with no protesting cries.

At eighty-five, Mother sifted the long-ago
from yellowed document and musty deed
to well-preserved, oft-repeated anecdote.
The town ancestors were etched in joy and woe
as they settled the village and planted seed.
Well-sifted notes shaped the history she wrote.

Mother still sifts time as once she sifted sand,
when a young girl by the gleaming lake shore,
although her first castles never kept dry,
she firmly rebuilt them on sturdier land.
At ninety, her hands keep searching for more,
her deep well-springs seem to bubble for aye!

THE ESSENCE OF MAN
(In Memory of My Friend Leo)

The sculptor chose him as a model
of man's fortitude
against the dark seasons
when the planter
can no longer plant,
and the builder can no longer build.

As the sculptor shaped plastic clay,
he firmly pressed in the furrows
plowed by pain,
and gently imprinted
the lesser lines of laughter.
With understanding heart
and supple fingers,
he shaped the deep, prophetic eyes,
and moulded the classic head of Leo.

This sculptured head evokes memories—
how patiently he waited,
discreetly chafing at the sharp bite
of pain that chastened him,
yet never once surrendering
before the race had ended.

His soul, reluctant to leave his loved ones,
hovered in the temple of his body
in those last brief hours.
Then, on the Feast of the Epiphany,

the gates of heaven opened wide,
and his spirit glided lightly
to a new beginning at God's side.

BEYOND CLOCKED TIME

The kiss is a sunburst
of radiant motion
when lovers floating
escape the earth
in luminous flight.
Can a kiss be captured
in intaglio of stone
or etched on a vase?
Will its secret yield
to chisel or brush?
Or will its dimension
remain unknown
except by lovers
exploring intimate worlds
beyond clocked time
and unlocked space!

AUTUMN IN VERMONT

This is a day that has been created
for timbrel and trumpet!
Swallows fly due south
while a daughter in Atlanta
watches her weather vane
steadily pointing north.
Running barefoot over
crushed velvet green,
she remembers
the sound of brittle leaves
crunching under new shoes,—
the sight of mountains glowing
with scarlet and bronze torches
beneath a sky of forget-me-not blue.
She remembers autumn in Vermont.
The scent of bonfires smoking,
and in the warmth of kitchen
the smells of supper cooking,
familiar faces smile then blur.
She promises herself:
''I'll return next autumn
when miracles unfold,
and hoard for my spirit's hunger
crisp coins of October gold!''

NIGHT SCENE

After fruitless attempts, when sleep would not be
    wooed
with its sweet release for a troubled spirit,
she arose in the cotton flannel darkness,
and gazed out of her window
at the sprawling, sleeping city.
High street lights spread an apricot glow,
while thick puffs of gunmetal smoke
ascended from dream-drunk households.
An aura of mystery clung to the scene,
and lent a touch of fantasy to the sleep-hungry hour.
Mounds of snow, decorated with icicles,
seemed like minarets transplanted
to city rooftops. From afar, she heard music—
as if magic horns and lutes could lure
the Prince to discover the captive Princess,
impatiently waiting for a hero's rescue.
Over the whole atmosphere, the peach-pink glaze
spun thickly like the frosting
on her thirtieth birthday cake.
She began to count the joys and sorrows
of her three decades. Her eyes were mesmerized
by the days and months floating in apricot haze
until her eyelids fluttered and closed,
and she found the comfort
of enchanted sleep.

FLOWER-FILLED FIELDS

Do you remember the summers of childhood,
brief as the music of grass whistles,
lost on the wind like puffs of dandelion?
We waded in fields of buttercups and daisies—
gently pulling each petal as we whispered
the magican incantation: ''loves me, loves me not,
loves me—.'' In the hazy heat of late July,
we picked an armful of ''brown-eyed Susans,''
our Mother's favorite daisy. How she smiled
as she held them close, and kissed our moist faces.
The dippers of cold sweet water she drew from the
   well
still taste sweet in my memory.

Those were flower-filled days of innocence
when we believed that everyone was kind.
Those were lazy days when we lay on our backs,
and watched the scudding clouds change shape.
   What joy
we found in the circus parading across the sky.

Only toward the end of that last summer
when we had to move in different directions,
were we to know the meaning of fear. Shivering
with the chill of foreboding, we put our arms
around each other for warmth and comfort.
Never were we to be together again, dear brother;
the consuming flames of war seared our souls
as you went to die in the infantry.

Bulldozers have long since scattered the petals
in the flower-filled fields of our childhood;
our farm is gone—the cold sweet well is dry.
Gone is the family—all but me—why? Why?
The wind answers with a keening cry!

A WHIFF OF WHIMSY

If I could launder all my days,
and wash the stains and spills away,
I wonder if I hung them out
upon the line to dry,
what grotesque shape would they assume
when whipped by storm and wind?
I can see each one ballooning out,
then stiffening and thinned—
ghosts with only one dimension—
shrunken and dim.

With spots and spills washed away,
I would not recognize these days—
no longer mine to spoil,
or even to enjoy.

NOT THE FINAL SUM

(In memory of Rev. Arthur Hewitt)

Like David he lived as a shepherd,
Tending his flocks both day and night,
And even as the ancient psalmist,
He found favor in the Lord's sight.

David could not build his temple,
But passed the task on to his son,
Our highland shepherd labored daily
That God's will on earth might be done.

When finally his eyes beheld
The steeple rising to the sky,
His prayers rang with gratitude:
"Glory to God Who dwells on high."

In times of anguish or small joys,
He played on the *"Harp of the North"*—
Exalting the work of the Lord—
Songs of rapture came pouring forth!

Then came that dark fall afternoon
When we stood on Cemetery Hill,
The gift God gave had been returned,
The silver voice and the harp were still.

From the depths we cried unto God:
"We bury your loving servant here,
Grant us comfort from our grief,
Give us one sign to vanquish fear."

The wind echoed with words of faith
As the sun escaped from a cloud;
"The grave is not the final sum,
Nor can song be stopped by a shroud."

MIDNIGHT OF MY SOUL

The clock tolls the midnight of my soul—
my heart knocks against my rib cage.
The street lies hushed—too deathly still
to break the beat of tom-toms
within my inner ear.
The thin mercurial piece of moon,
half obscured
by a swiftly floating cloud,
reminds me of God's eye,
viewing the mixed-up human scene,
whether swaddling babe or final shroud.
I pull the shade,
and slide into my still half-empty bed,
silent as the grave.
My sorrow blends with the darkness.
Tears and prayers yield to soothing dreams
of earth bedecked with flowers.

PROPHECY

The tendrils of my vine
entwine around your trunk
as if toward sun.
Your skin feels smooth and supple,
yet unyielding
to my touch.
A chill envelops me.
I sense you wish to remove
the tendrils of my vine,
so long accustomed
to growing around you,
as if toward sun.

When tendrils of a living
vine can no longer find
a support on which to twine
its searching tendrils die.
And so shall I.

BEFORE THE DIVORCE:
PERHAPS—

Before we write *finis* to the book
we wrote together,
let us climb one more mountain,
regardless of the weather;
gather one more bouquet of daisies,
and forget the rue.
Let's race barefoot in the fields
wet with morning dew.
We could hold each other close all day,
and through the hushed night,
until the meadow lark's song
awakens us to sunlight.
We might breakfast on wild strawberries,
and feel Cupid's dart,
then write another chapter,
and forget to part.

ONCE IN THE LONG AGO NURSERY

Through the upstairs window she sees
the random heaping of the leaves,
and above the soughing wind,
hears echoes of children's happy cries,
even the weathered rocking chair
creaks with the hum of lullabies.
A Mother's heart twists against the ropes
tied by time and too many miles.

From the Maples' bright vermillion,
aflame in the chill autumnal air,
one glowing ember rekindles
smouldering dreams and hopes.
Her eyes smile as her mind predicts
that soon grandchildren will come
holding a handful
of daffodil sun!

ETUDE IN GRAY

No flaming sunset lightens the clouds
at the end of this dismal day.
Against the thick white shrouds,
pencil gray trees stretch tall
and the road slithers away
like an elusive eel
as darkness falls.
Ringed by twenty-five years, we ride
over slippery country roads
enveloped in twilight gray,
and listen for the gurgle
of gunmetal streams,
but brooks lie mute
in the charcoal night.
Windshield wipers drone—
a mesmerizing metronome—
like Alice I shrink smaller
at each succeeding tick.
I feel isolated,
unloved and unwanted,
a victim of mouse-gray blight.

Then one of your hands slips from the wheel
and firmly touches my own.
Your gentle touch reminds me
that I need not feel
alone.

AS GRACIOUSLY AS SHE HAD LIVED

Her apron tied neatly still to her
polished maple chair,
the copper kettle gleaming,
her prize-winning African violets
exuberant with blossoms,
the slender vases glinted amber
in the sunlight pouring
through freshly washed glass,
and crisp curtains, firmly tied back—
Aunt Grace had left us as graciously
as she had always lived.

We found her lying under the fruit
laden apple tree, she looked
peaceful as if taking a respite
from her daily labor.
Above her in the branches,
robins and song sparrows
chanted litanies of love
for one who daily fed them
sunflower seeds and pieces
of homebaked honey bread.

IN QUEST OF HER SLEEP

All night she lay awake
hearing the quarter hour chime
from midnight until dawn.
How she longed and prayed
that time could be charmed
not chimed.
When the stiletto of dawn
began to peel
the darkness from the sky,
her eyes were finally disarmed
by sleep, and all the clocks
temporarily consigned
to the briny deep.

BLUE MAGIC

What is there about a blue, blue sky
that makes one want to fly?
Or sail away with the wind
steering red sails through the seven seas?
Or ride a unicorn
through velveteen fields
with never a car in view?
There's something magic
in a blue, blue sky
that makes the child
in me reply.

SPRING OFFERING

When the first crocus of spring
boldly pokes its pastel petals
through dead leaves,
I remember a tall man
with a white moustache,
and twinkling blue eyes.
Happy as a schoolboy
on a holiday, he picked
the first crocus,
and with a courtly flourish
presented it to grandmother.

BEYOND MERE WORDS

Some events seem too big, too bright,
Too bold and beautiful
For mere words to enhance.
Some days, too full-blown and bountiful
To be ascribed to chance.

Some evenings grow too blossom-filled,
Too blissful and beneficent
For more than bated breath.
Some boys bloom into men more blessed
Than mere words can attest.

NOT OURS TO KEEP

I know there can never be candlelight
Enough to penetrate the awesome dark,
Where each must dwell in the realm of midnight.
Before that too swift hushing of the lark,
Let me hold your hand and run, dearest friend,
Where the clearing ends and the woods begin.
Time is not ours to keep, yet past the bend,
the Ice King may be life's fraternal twin.

Like Hansel and Gretel we enter the wood—
Fearful of witches and shadowy shapes,
We tremble lest one who wears shroud and hood
Might seduce our hunger with poison grapes.

We hold each other—with love we are braced,
At dawn I can see all your pain is erased.

A LEGEND OF THE MOUNTAINS

My cousin's bride
      (newly arrived from the prairie) cried:
"These hostile high mountains hem me in,
Glowering at me as if I am an alien,
And they are alien indeed to me.
Let me go home where the land rolls free,
And earth and sky make one horizon."

With all the deep compassion
That my thirteen years could summon,
The pride of five generations of Vermonters
Rising to my tongue, I solemnly replied:
"Cousin Joan, anyone with sense can see
Our Green Mountains are friendly giants,
Protecting our valley from the evil beyond."

      Her tears would not be denied.
      Nor foolish fears allayed.
      "Good God, child," she sobbed,
      "For all that lies beyond your mountains,
      My very soul is weeping."

I dared not speak again
      (bitter words are best unsaid),
I bit my lips until they bled.
My beloved cousin, considerate of his chosen wife,
Simply had to settle for a dull prairie life.

Months and years swirled like mountain snow,
I was eighteen when Grandmother confided:
"I'm getting near the end, and rightly so,
Your Grandfather is waiting for me,
And he never was a patient man, you know.
My dearest comfort now that I am useless
Is looking up at our mountains. I cannot
Fill my eyes enough with their green promise.
When I die, I feel certain God will lift me up!"

My cousin and his wife came for the funeral.
I was reading Grandmother's Bible,
Open as usual at the 121st Psalm,
When Joan spoke softly: "I'm home—
Home to stay, and no nonsense, I've missed
Your friendly giants too much," she smiled.
I laid the Bible on the table. Suddenly it shut.
I heard Grandmother's voice say clearly:
"Now the knife of parting can no longer cut,
Lift up your eyes and rejoice!"

THIS APRIL TWILIGHT

I simply refuse
to say farewell like this—
with you against your will
inching away from me
farther and farther each day—
your eyes no longer open
wide-eyed like a little boy
who slowly licks a lemon lollypop
trying to make it last and last.

I've always wanted,
my darling, for us to leave
together on an ocean liner
with all flags flying
and drinking toasts
with champagne chilled
in a silver bucket.
No plastic glasses for us
but ringing crystal
that we could drain
and hurl joyfully,
defiantly crying:
"L'Chayim—to Life!"

There is no ordinary way
that we can separate
in this April twilight.
Let me take your hand
and together

we will find
an open door
to our inescapable
beginning!

LILACS IN THE RAIN

I don't know anything more lovely
than lilacs in the rain,
and you, helping me choose
the half-open ones, magenta hued.
Savoring lilac kisses,
laughing at the shower,
we plunge our faces in the fresh cool,
breathe in the heady fragrance.

Surely, in the life that comes after,
nothing can be lovelier
than the sound of laughter,
as lovers gather
lilacs in the rain.

SUNSET OVER HONOLULU BAY

Always at the setting of the sun
When the ocean turns to pirate gold,
I hear the guitars and native songs
of our melodious Hawaii.
As the dusk descends,
I relive the ritual
we shared—
the arresting notes
of the Conch Shell,
blown by the royal Chieftain.
The runners carry the flame
to light the ceremonial torches,
and then the Festival of Night
begins with undulating dance,
and sensuous song.
I remember, yes, I remember well
those days when you were here,
and nothing in my world was wrong.

RAINBOWS OF HAWAII

Oahu, island of rainbows—
promise of paradise regained,
whenever it rains leeward,
rainbows leap from the sky,
and arch above the clouds.
It is then I see
all the sorrows in your eyes
eclipsed by rainbows.
Your eyes shimmer and mist
with the joy of being alive
like the orchids of Oahu,
blessed by the singing rain.

SHATTERED SABBATH

I rose in joy at the pinking sheared sky—
a dawn of delight—
the dew kissed lilacs scented the day
with their fresh fragrance.
God's covenant seemed alive
in the shimmering light!
Song sparrows and robins peeled away
the last grey shreds of night
with their melodic blessings.
The Sabbath morning blossom filled
with pink-purple and white lilac May.

My feet turned aside from the House of Prayer,
where I might drink from the freshets of
Torah, and led me instead to the House of
Commerce where another day's work awaited.
The secular and the profane ensnare my soul.
Although the heavens should open up
by God's own volition,
for me, there is no balm of Gilead.
Nowhere is there an ointment sweet
enough to heal the wounds
of my shattered Sabbath.

PRAYER FOR JERUSALEM

The bronze sun began its glittering descent
behind the scorched Judean hills,
and I walked as if in a dream
over the historic cobblestones
of old Jerusalem, city of gold!
My pulse quickened as I finally arrived
at the sacred Western Wall.
As I placed my hands upon the temple stones,
I felt at one with every pilgrim,
who poured faith, hope and tears
upon this eternal remnant.
A magnetic current surged
through every nerve.

Humbly at first, then louder and more daring,
the voices around me rose
in a crescendo of tear-stained exaltation
to assault the very gates of heaven.
I joined the chorus pleading
for Shalom for Jerusalem,
and for the descendants of Isaac and Ishmael,
that they might live side by side,
and savor the sweet fruits
of peace and brotherhood.

MORNING BALLET

Early risers in the first pink of morning
slowly scrub sleep from eyes
still steeped in poppy dreams,
and pristine dark.
A cup of hot brew—a hasty devouring
of headlines—then the day's ballet begins.
Early risers meld into the growing company
moving with a rhythm
that no one dares resist.
As the choreography unfolds,
the mood elevates.
The members buoyant now. Each moves
onward to a separate role.
Collectively, and alone,
all and each feels touched
by the irresistible movement
of morning
with a meaning unmistakably
its very own!

A LETTER TO EMILY OF AMHERST

Dear Emily, today I'll walk with you,
We'll bear glad witness to the singing sun,
And watch the robins sipping morning dew,
Raise coffee mugs to toast the poems you've spun,
And mark the passage of the slithering snake.
We'll feast on slices of fresh honey bread
While the summer flees in his witching wake,
Poetry and preserves will season our spread.

Oh, how I pray such communion might last—
Too soon, the clouds glow pink with the sunset
For clock hands still move unfeelingly fast,
Ending a day I will never forget.

As rose-gold and mauve suffuse every cloud,
Your poignant words keep my spirit unbowed.

THE QUESTION BEGS AN ANSWER

Whatever can be the reason
that good men die young?
Their loved ones left
to wonder why
the wicked ride
on a high horse
with a dubious
lie upon their tongue.

Why do the good die young?
A question more than thrice
repeated because
there are too many wars,
and those in high places
must have their wars
as did the ancient gods
their human sacrifice.

The sun goes down at day's end
in purple pomp
behind the everlasting hills,
but where do they rest
who die skull-shattered
jaws locked forever
in the grip of death?

Where do their bones rest now—
those innocents
napalm cindered?

Those maidens starved
in their maidenhood
like tightly closed rosebuds
never unfurled?

Where do they rest, these young men,
the arteries and veins
of every nation,
now blown away, gone
before their pulse
could quicken in the
umbilical cutting
joy of fatherhood?

Why do they die before they should?
Is it because
the computer clocks
of the war-makers
are running to the zero hour,
and taking our world
into oblivion,
before a new generation
can recreate
the human race
in the image of
a God who loves?

THE BOY WHO WHISTLED IN THE DARK
*(In Memory of 241 U.S. Marines Killed in Beirut,
Lebanon in October, 1983)*

There once was a red-haired boy with freckles
who always whistled in the dark—
his hands in his pockets,
lips all puckered up,
his sea-green eyes, serious yet sparkling.
Should he meet some ferocious monster,
he would mesmerize it
with a long, hypnotic gaze.
All the while, he whistled nursery melodies
to hold his fears at bay.

Celebrating his eighteenth birthday,
he enlisted in that legendary Corps,
the United States Marines.
Wearing his uniform with proper pride,
he sailed away to an alien land.
The Mission? Simply, "to keep the peace."
In between the rocket blasts and shell-fire,
he often whistled the melodies
of childhood and carousel days.
His buddies called his whistling,
"a kind of praying."

Then came that Sunday morning
as he cradled his rifle at the sentry post,
when the "suicide" truck came hurtling by.
He fired, but no bullet could hold

that explosive monster at bay.
He remembered that unbearable feeling
of absolute helplessness,
when he escorted the bodies of his comrades
back home to the aching hearts,
and empty arms of their loved ones.

When the bugler played "Taps" the heavens seemed
to split open, as if all the angels spilled
their tears upon the anguished earth.
The little boy, now grown into a tall Marine,
felt his tears gush forth from a bursting dam.
Fear, no longer a make-believe monster, but death,
a reality unwanted, unwelcomed,
and totally inescapable. At last he cried out:
"Surrender? Never." He began to whistle softly
the Marine Anthem: "From the Halls of Montezuma
to the shores of Tripoli...."

THE FIRST COMING

The first snowfall arrives bountifully
with the music of muted trumpets.
Sleepy children snuggled under their blankets
tingle with anticipation—
dream of snowballs squishing
against houses and autos,
and squashing perilously close
to the surprised faces of adults
toppling their hats and their dignity.

Mothers go hunting in dresser drawers, and
assorted boxes for mittens and scarves.
Then they look through the window
at autumn's leavings covered with white
including the garden chores left undone,
and the children's toys still in the yard.

After cars are moved from street to driveway,
fires are kindled, and lumpy figures
in soft slippers and robes
slump nodding as they forget
the need for shoveling, and dream
of being children once again.

Young lovers holding hands run
with mouths open, tongues out
to taste the fresh-falling flakes.
With rollicking laughter, they lie down
to shape the season's first snow angels.

Everyone steadily refuses
to desecrate the first coming
by disloyal thoughts of subzero
temperatures, ice slick roads,
and other such attendant inconveniences.

THE LINGERING LIGHT

Long after the winter solstice,
before the April leaves unfurl,
and daffodils lift up their trumpets,
there comes a promise
annually fulfilled—
the perceptible strengthening
and lengthening of daylight.
My pulse quickens,
the tide of my blood rises
in waves of alleluias.

As winter's wafer light
elongates and expands,
the burdens on my mind
fall swiftly as the shades
of last December.
I embrace the lingering light!
I would hold it forever
in my eyes,
but such joy can never
long endure
this side of paradise!

LONG NIGHT AND MORNING STAR
(For Georgianna)

All night she made the rounds in the dark
moving noiselessly and easily
in and out of rooms
where patients half-dozing
waited for a glimpse
of her white uniform
and brown eyes glistening
in the small arc of flashlight.
Her soft voice gentled the terror
of tomorrow's operation,
and afterwards, pain diminished
beneath the touch
of her healing fingers.
Sensing the loneliness
she paused and spoke
everyday words bright
as newly minted coin
while she turned pillows and rubbed backs.
She looked out the window
as the clock turned
toward the edge of dawn
and saw the rising
of the Morning Star.
As she began the litany
to Mary Regina, Most Radiant
of heaven's morning stars,
her tired feelings vanished.

She prayed for all the sick and lonely
that their long night
would open into morning!

THE LEGACY OF LIGHT

Outside, wild January storms!
Inside, the dark of winter
magically dispelled
as the mistress of the castle
lovingly performs
the ritual of lamps.
Ever since the legacy of light
was first passed on
from mother to daughter
in the firelit cave,
woman hums a lilting tune
as she pulls the drapes against
the sullen, hostile night,
and floods her rooms
with friendly pools of light.

Scents of supper spice the air,
the kettle bubbles, the glass gleams.
Telltale footsteps at the door—
she peers into the mirror—
quite satisfied, she glides
regal as any queen to greet
her ''equal,'' the prince-consort
of her lamplit castle.

THE SHARING

Fleeing from tightly scheduled hours,
and relentless Freeway weaving,
we three, my son and Kyoko and I,
arrived at the ocean shore
for the ceremony of sharing
a Pacific sunset.

We sipped our iced drinks and waited—
separately and yet together—
I, from the Western world,
Kyoko from the Orient,
and my son from the bridge
where West and East have met.

As the sun began to descend,
it glowed with rose-red fire
like an oversized Japanese lantern.
We watched in reverent silence
as the gigantic lantern turned
into a globe of molten gold,
diminishing, gradually,
into a glittering plate that slipped
without a splash into the sea.
All that remained were the fish
leaping in arcs of light,
until they too, disappeared.

We glimpsed a peaceful universe
beyond tumult and turmoil;

We forgot the hectic day's toil,
and satisfied the famished soul.

OF INTERLUDES AND INTRUSIONS

Sometimes, she pauses and sighs in the midst
of her multiple, mundane tasks—
picking up the children's toys,
washing diapers, scrubbing the floor—
to steal precious moments for daydreams.
As she leans back on her heels on the hard
linoleum, in her imagination,
she's reclining on a satin cushion.
Her loving mate brings her a bowl
of fresh strawberries, generously splashed
with pink champagne. Music plays pianissimo—
no disconcerting cries. She savors
each berry with a connoisseur's delight.
Abruptly, the baby awakens with a howl,
the children intrude noisily from school.
The kitchen floor is still half washed,
the water not even lukewarm.
Slowly she moves to her feet, well aware
that time can not be checked for long.
Although, she can almost taste the fruit
laced with champagne, and hear the echo
of soothing song, her hands reach out
yearning once more to secure
her satin-textured interlude.

FORGOTTEN?

Toboggan rides under the frosty stars—
our bodies tilting perilously close
to the steep, dark banks,
then the crunch of our boots in unison
as we began the long haul back.
There were moon-drenched nights
when we skated on the glass
of our secret cove.
Later, laughing and shivering, we built a fire,
melted snow, and devoured mugs of hot cocoa—
only our silences tasted more delicious
than sugar-spun conversation.
You promised when spring arrived
we'd go flowering in our hidden woods
for arbutus, hepaticas, and violets.

Now, today, when April crossed the threshold,
I've knocked on every emerald door,
and can't even find your thumbprint.
They tell me you've left our village
with only your backpack,
yet, I know for sure
you carry excess baggage—
the quicksilver of all my dreams!

BEYOND THE DARKNESS

Here at the edge of darkness,
I still hold on
to the needle-sharp rim
of reality.
The cliffs seem to rise
on every side
to hem me in.
I hear the rapids rushing
far below,
their roar drowns my cries—
a testing of the soul.

Dawn finds me
still holding on.
My bleeding hands remind me
that reality is won
through a willingness
to hold fast
beyond the darkness,
past the spokes
of dawn!

BEFORE THE STARS GO OUT

Scene 1.

Would that we might meet with laughter
one thousand days from today—
forgetting there ever was or could be
a parting of our way.
Would that we might see our daughter
radiant as a bride,
and all the sorrows of the past
swept away by the tide—
the rolling tide of happiness
that comes once to us all.
Would that we might dance with laughter,
and wear love like a paisley shawl!

Scene 2.

We can not parry any longer,
the day has vanished,
the sunset bled,
the night well worn
past midnight.
Let us slip into the deep sea
of undulating sleep,
and forget there will be
a final night—
that no one can circumvent—
when even this sea lies still.
Before the stars go out,
let us float
across the mythical moat
into Avalon.

LINES TO BAT SHEVA

Bat Sheva, daughter of seven,
daughter of the Shabbas Malke,
grand-daughter of our gathering years,
tonight we heard you sing—
and it was different from all other nights,
for tonight you sang
in Yiddish!
The mameloshen seemed
sweet as honey
rolling lyrically
from your tongue.
You sang with the joy
of one who knows how
to open the day with song;
you sang with all the pride
of a nine year old
whose roots grow deep
in our people's history.
In your sweet, clear voice
there pulsed the heart of your ancestors
who lived, loved and even dreamed
in Yiddish.
The world they built
block by block
vanished in fire and smoke.
Only tonight, you retrieved
that lost world for us,
and the frozen stars began to thaw.

This morning I awoke,
my face, humid with hot tears—
I could hear your voice singing—
raising our half-forgotten hope
that the little ones who sang
in the darkness of the ghettos,
in the rubble of destruction,
will live again,
will sing again
with your voice.

THE QUESTIONING

Can I celebrate
the lark on the wing
shot in mid-flight—
rounded hosannas
abruptly hushed?

Can I celebrate
the trout on the hook
losing the fight
its leaping in sunlight
suddenly stilled?

Can I celebrate
the child in the street
under heavy wheels
still holding her kite—
curly head crushed?

But, I can celebrate
my husband's delight
after the dark of pain
when our Shoshana
sings him a morning
melody filled!

DOUBLE CINQUAIN

The Last Scene

> Our lives
> ran together
> we two built a staunch house,
> one that lightning did not destroy—
>
> Our house,
> the home we built
> toppled into the sea;
> while the bell buoy tolled a warning,
> Death grinned.

The Last Sunset

> My love
> gasped his good-bye;
> the four children and I
> replied, ''Please, rest in peace, dear one,
> Shalom.''
>
> The sun
> bathed Mansfield's crown
> with liquid, golden light—
> his life blood ebbing swirled in rose
> sunset.

THE LAST ANNIVERSARY

This November night unfolded with stars;
even heaven's doors seemed to open wide;
short decades ago, we stood trembling
on the threshold of our wedding night.
Since that time, we two have scaled the ropes
of Jacob's ladder hand over hand—
feeling the same fears—
lost in the elusive light.
Our palms and feet bear the scars
of the scalding rope burns,
yet we climbed on
when our limbs rebelled.
Now, poised just below the zenith,
we wait—almost ready for the final ascent.
The frosty stars blaze like celestial candles
blessing our anniversary,
we hear again the guitars and violins
playing our love song;
after thirty-two years, we are lifted up
in the starstruck light
of one last full-blown November night.

ONE FRAGRANT MOMENT

Only four o'clock by the owlwise
clock on the dimly lit Diner wall.
The darkness outside is spreading
and squeezing my heart.
I go out in the street,
and see huge honeycombs of light
in the towering office buildings.
People in warm down coats
and woolen wear
scurry briskly to and fro.
Each head bristles with Christmas lists.
Gifts in shop windows
whirl and swirl
in a kaleidoscope of color.
Sequins sparkle
silver and gold
tinsel and glitter!
Carols churn the air,
coins fill pseudo-Santa's pots.
Beyond the shops
and the milling shoppers,
there is our home.
I run up the hill
and hurry fast to greet you,
forgetting
for one fragrant moment
that you are no longer
there to comfort me.

THIS DIFFERENT APRIL

Incredible that April has come once more
with all her usual insouciance!
She has arrived—our month of months
for whom we always longed and waited.
As the wheel spun and the green-
growing season turned and returned,
we drank deeply from the wells of love,
and renewed our vows. Only *this* Spring,
you are not here.
My pulse slows as tears salt
my widow's weeds.
I listen to the music of April—
more plaintive than before—
the woodwinds wail,
the cellos moan,
the brass, muted.
Then, above the lament, the sweet,
clear notes of the flutes begin
their affirmation:
"There is no death,
there is no stone
that can hold the spirit
beneath the earth."
I seem to feel a gentle wind—
the breath of your soul.
Though I must cry alone,
I still believe
in April and the flutes.